THE HALL OF GEOGRAPHICAL MAPS IN PALAZZO VECCHIO

caprice and invention of Duke Cosimo

Edizioni Polistampa

THE HALL OF GEOGRAPHICAL MAPS IN PALAZZO VECCHIO
CAPRICE AND INVENTION OF DUKE COSIMO

Edited by
Paola Pacetti

Texts
Paola Pacetti and Valentina Zucchi,
The Hall of Geographical Maps or Wardrobe in Palazzo Vecchio
Massimo Marcolin with Monica Consoli,
The wonders *of the Hall of Geographical Maps in Palazzo Vecchio*

Editorial secretariat
Monica Consoli with Roberta Masucci and Lorenzo Valloriani

Illustrations
Studio Ink Link

Photographs
Domingie & Rabatti Photographers, Florence; Studio Fotografico Tosi, Florence;
Bencini Raffaello Studio Fotografico, Florence

Planning, editing and printing
Edizioni Pagliai Polistampa

© 2014 Edizioni Polistampa
   Via Livorno, 8/32 - 50142 Florence
   Tel. 055 737871 (15 lines)
   info@polistampa.com - www.polistampa.com

ISBN 978-88-596-1446-3

PRESENTATION

Some of the first results of extensive research carried out in 2005-06 by a broadly interdisciplinary work team on the Hall of Geographical Maps in Palazzo Vecchio (Sala delle Carte geografiche) are presented here. This hall contains the Western World's oldest and certainly most important representation of the whole known world in the second half of the sixteenth century – thanks to the invention and caprice of Duke Cosimo and the intelligent action of Giorgio Vasari, assisted by the court cosmographers, Don Miniato Pitti and Friar Egnazio Danti.

In today's society it has been nearly forgotten that Italy, up to the seventeenth century, possessed the greatest amount of information on the functioning of the whole world, more than all the other countries put together. And yet we need only think of what still exists in the palaces of our cities: Rome, Venice, Genoa and, above all, Florence. Hence it is unsurprising that a Hall planned as an amazing display of knowledge should be constructed in Florence, in the Palace symbolic of the city. Based on a program for representing as a whole the "things of heaven and earth just as they are and without errors", this Hall constituted the key to and conclusion of the grand-ducal iconographic project conceived by Cosimo and implemented by Vasari. But despite its scientific importance and the fascination it holds for visitors, the Hall had never before been subjected to specific studies aimed at understanding the motivations behind the original project, the reasons for its partial abandonment, and the subsequent construction of the Terrace of Mathematics in the Galleria degli Uffizi, frescoed with maps of the grand-ducal state at the order of Grand Duke Ferdinando I.

Giovanni Gozzini
Councillor for Cultural Affairs for the City of Florence

THE SIDE OF PALAZZO VECCHIO OVERLOOKING VIA DELLA NINNA

THE ROOMS IN PALAZZO VECCHIO
(opposite page)

1. Audience Chamber
2. Hall of Lilies
3. Hall of Geographical Maps
4. Hall of the Five Hundred
5. Hall of the Elements
6. Terrace of Saturn
7. Mezzanine
8. Michelozzo's Courtyard
9. Studiolo of Francesco I
10. Treasury of Cosimo I
11. Hall of Leo X
12. Hall of Clement VII

The original fourteenth-century core, attributed to Arnolfo di Cambio, overlooking the piazza. Faced in massive rustication and crowned by a crenellated guard and a tower 95 meters high

Overhead passageway above Via della Ninna joining Palazzo Vecchio to the Uffizi, and opening into the Vasari Corridor

Today's Hall of the Five Hundred, or Salone dei Cinquecento, formerly Sala del Consiglio Maggiore: built at the initiative of Savonarola in the late 15th century, it was transformed by Vasari into the Sala Grande

New apartments ordered by Cosimo I and built by Battista del Tasso in the second half of the 16th century

The Hall of Geographical Maps or Wardrobe in Palazzo Vecchio

Who does not know Palazzo Vecchio, which – with its crenellated walls surmounted by an imposing tower – overlooks Piazza della Signoria in Florence? Depicted in innumerable views of the city, it is one of Florence's best-known icons.

It is harder to answer the question of what Palazzo Vecchio is. It is certainly a noble monument, seat of the city's government since the fourteenth century, as shown by its architectural aspect. But the visitor entering Michelozzo's Courtyard from the entrance on Piazza della Signoria discovers a style that pertains no longer to the medieval past, but to the full sixteenth century. After passing through Michelozzo's Courtyard and climbing the broad staircase to enter, first, the Hall of the

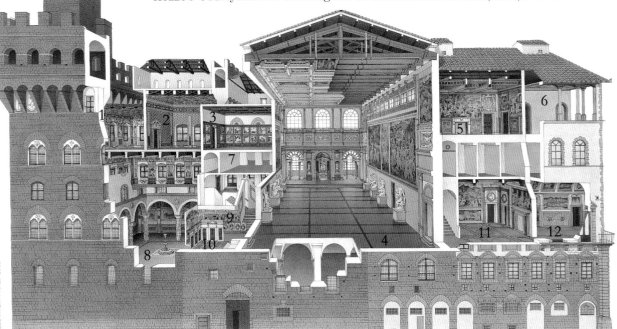

Five Hundred and from there the Apartment of Leo X, then those of the Elements and of Eleonora, the Audience Chamber, the Hall of Lilies and lastly the Hall of Geographical Maps, we find ourselves in the ducal Palace built to the order of Cosimo I de' Medici in the second half of the sixteenth century. Palazzo Vecchio is thus a sort of two-faced herm, and the first Medicean ducal palace appears almost hidden behind the massive medieval walls.

This dual nature of the Palace can be traced directly to Cosimo I de' Medici, who upon becoming duke at a very early ago, not yet eighteen, in 1540 – after having married Eleonora di Toledo, daughter of the Viceroy of Naples – decided to live in the *Palazzo di Piazza*, in keeping with his political aim of maintaining continuity with the city's glorious republican past, while simultaneously affirming and consolidating his own absolute power. But the political acumen behind the young Duke's decision to move with his family to the Palace also led him to request Georgio Vasari *"not to alter the foundations and the maternal walls of this place, since it is this old form that has given rise to his new government..."*[1]

This first Medicean ducal palace, built within the *maternal walls* of Palazzo dei Priori, derived not only from the order of Duke Cosimo – as *strong-willed client* – but also from the work of Giorgio Vasari, who was to be its *multivalent director* from 1555 to his death in 1574, two months after that of the Duke.

Vasari strove to attain a decorum combining his technical knowledge as treatise writer with construction strategies and the utilization of artisans specialized in all fields (glass, wood, stucco, terracotta and, above all tapestry) to produce a grandiose celebratory project that would fully legitimate Cosimo and his government. Contributing to the development of this program were Florence's most eminent scholars. Cosimo's political decision obliged Vasari to operate in extremely difficult conditions, of which the artist was fully aware when he noted that *"many are those who have made new buildings, beautifully decorated and admirable, and this is unsurprising; but he who takes a twisted, ruined body and transforms it into healthy, straight limbs possesses miraculous skill.*[2]

It should be noted that when Vasari entered the Duke's service in 1555, Cosimo had already victoriously concluded the war against Siena and could now – being certain of the solidity of his state and his own policies – focus new attention on the Palace, seat of the court and the family. From 1555 to 1565, in fact, the architectural work was strikingly accelerated, while at the same time the entire decorative

[1] Giorgio Vasari, *Ragionamenti*, Giornata prima, Ragionamento primo, Florence 1588, p. 4

[2] Ivi, p. 1

programme of the Hall, featuring Cosimo and his government as the heroes of the stories painted on the ceilings and walls, was planned and implemented, giving rise to mythological cycles, as in the Apartment of the Elements; historical cycles, as in the Apartment of Leo X and the Hall of the Five Hundred; and geographical cycles, as in the Hall of Maps, which represents the completion of the entire decorative project.

The decorative scheme for the Hall of Maps was in fact planned, in 1562-63, by the Duke himself in collaboration with Vasari and with the contribution of Friar Miniato Pitti, Vasari having decided to built a sort of loggia adjoining the Hall of Lilies, which was then to become the first Hall of the Wardrobe, the heart of the

G. Vasari, *Cosimo I surrounded by artists*, Hall of Cosimo I (1556), Palazzo Vecchio

Medicean court, where all of the movable property of the State and the grand-ducal family was safeguarded.

It is important to note that the Hall of Geographical Maps had, like the Palace itself, a dual nature. It was in fact both Wardrobe ("*On the second floor of the rooms in his ducal palace, His Excellency with the order of Vasari has had newly built and added to the wardrobe a very large room, and has placed tall cabinets all around it... richly inlaid in walnut, to keep there the most important, most valuable and most beautiful things His Excellency owns*") and Hall of Geographical Maps: "*the doors of said cabinets are decorated with 57 pan-*

The Hall of Geographical Maps
seen from the Audience Chamber,
Palazzo Vecchio

els... in which are... painted in oil Ptolemy's tables, all perfectly dimensioned and corrected according to the new authors and with the correct navigation charts..."[3] and the different weights and measures of these two functions over the course of history not only accompanied, but even seem to anticipate future changes in the reign of Cosimo and in the palace, during the process in which it became "Old" over the course of the seventeenth century.

The Hall of Geographical Maps, "this caprice and invention conceived by Duke Cosimo to bring together all of the things of Heaven and Earth most correctly and without error..."[4] represented the highest celebration of the Duke's power, since the whole scheme of the Hall was aimed at symbolizing the dominion of the cosmos over the world – also through the coupled names, Cosimo/Cosmos. As such, it demonstrated how the perfection with which God has ordained the whole universe is a privilege reserved to he who has received directly from God the right to govern. Today, visitors to the Monumental Apartments find:

• fifty-three panels, thirty of them painted by Egnazio Danti and twenty by the Olivetan monk Stefano Buonsignori;

• the great terrestrial globe, measuring two meters and ten centimeters in diameter, constructed by Friar Egnazio, at the centre of the room.

But the original configuration of this hall was very different: the celestial constellations painted on the ceiling; the bases of the cabinets decorated with images of the flora and fauna of each territory; and above the cabinets, busts of the emperors and princes who had governed the various lands, along with portraits of three hundred illustrious men from the last five centuries. Against the wall, facing the entrance, was a planetary clock, while the Duke's guests, as they approached the Hall, would have seen descending from the panels in the ceiling two great globes: a terrestrial one that came to rest on the floor and a celestial one that remained suspended above it, to symbolize the domination of the cosmos over the world.

It was not the changing fortunes of history, from the 16th century to our own day, to disperse and destroy the other elements in the project; on the contrary, it was abandoned almost at once, as soon as the legitimation of Cosimo's government had been fully attained by political means: in 1565 with the wedding of his son Francesco to the daughter of the Emperor of Austria, and above all in 1570, when Cosimo was crowned Grand Duke of Tuscany. In this change of direction, the role of Francesco played a major part.

[3] Giorgio Vasari, *Le vite dei più eccellenti pittori, scultori e architettori; Degl'accademici del disegno pittori, scultori et architetti e dell'opere loro e prima del Bronzino*, tome II, Florence 1568, p. 877

[4] Ivi, p. 878

The Hall of Geographical Maps,
E. Danti (1563-75) and
S. Buonsignori (1576-86),
Palazzo Vecchio

Already in his capacity as regent, starting in 1564, he saw no need to continue with the celebratory art that distinguished the entire decoration of the palace and had been designed to culminate in the great cosmic machine of the Hall of Maps. A very different political context, a diversity of interests and taste, the deterioration of his relationship with Giorgio Vasari, all contributed within a few years' time to make the project for the Hall of Maps and, more generally, the whole Ducal

Palace, of little interest to Francesco. Upon becoming Grand Duke in 1574, he determinedly pursued new artistic goals that led him to the realization, among other things, of that encyclopedia of wonders known as the Tribuna of the Uffizi.

Accordingly, in the Hall of Geographical Maps, the painted panels were completed only in 1586, while Danti's great globe was not placed in the Hall but first in Palazzo Pitti's Hall of the Globe (*Sala dell'mappamondo*) and then, around 1594, on the Terrace of Mathematics (*Terrazzo delle matematiche*) in the Galleria degli Uffizi, which the new Grand Duke, Ferdinando I, then had decorated with maps of the Tuscan territorial state established by Cosimo.

To our contemporary eyes the Hall today, although downsized from the original project to include only the maps on the cabinet doors, constitutes an extraordinary document of geographical knowledge in the second half of the 16th century. But to the eyes of those who lived and worked in the Palace near the end of that century, its function and reason for being depended not on the presence of those maps, become, so to say, *opaque*, but on its role as central Hall in the Medicean Wardrobe Apartment. This is clearly shown by the inventories of the Wardrobe – where the court officials noted with extreme care the entire heritage safeguarded in all of the rooms used for this purpose – since the geographical maps painted on the cabinet doors were never utilized to identify their contents. It is confirmed still further by the names adopted for the room itself: "*New room of the clock*[5], *Main room of the Wardrobe*[6], *Second Room of the Wardrobe*[7]" and – from the end of the 16th century up to and throughout the 18th – "*Silver Plate Room*[8]".

The Hall, in fact, formed part of the Wardrobe Apartment (*Quartiere di Guardaroba*) which was transformed over the years in relation to the needs of the court, gradually expanding, first into rooms assigned to this purpose and later – starting from the 17th century and mainly in the 18th – into formerly residential and representational areas. Supervising these possessions was a real Wardrobe Department, responsible not only for administering the family's possessions but also for commissioning furniture, objects, and everything found necessary by the court. Subordinate to this department were all the others: the armory, the foundry, the stables, the pantry, the wine-bottlers and tapestry-weavers.

Over them all reigned the Keeper of the Wardrobe, who held a powerful, prestigious role, being responsible for supervising the operations and functioning of the Department and choosing the suppliers to be used at his own discretion. Entrusted with an immense economic heritage, the Keeper of the Wardrobe was held per-

[5] Archivio di Stato di Firenze (ASF), Guardaroba Medicea, Inventory of His Majesty's Wardrobe, March 1570, f. 73, c. 52 ss.

[6] ASF, Guardaroba Medicea, General Inventory of the Wardrobe of His Most Serene Highness the Grand Duke of Tuscany Franc.o Medici the Second, November 1587 - January 1588, c. 68r

[7] *Ibidem*

[8] ASF, Guardaroba Medicea, General Register of Wardrobe Items, February 1608 – f. 289, c. 39 ff.; ASF, Guardaroba Medicea, Inventory of the Wardrobe, September 1637-August 1638, f. 521, c. 20r

View of the Palace with the little external "corridor", 1848, Museo Storico Topografico "Firenze com'era"

sonally responsible for anything missing. Assisted by his subordinates, he had to guarantee a constant presence in the Apartment, day and night, to safeguard the content of the rooms and be able to respond to any nocturnal request.

And in the Palace of today, what has survived of this great Apartment? The rooms remain, devoid of their functions and occupied mainly by the offices of the City Government, while the objects once kept there are now to be found in many Florentine museums, often forming the oldest core of the collections. But if we go back in time, attempting to trace the history of the Wardrobe Apartment, we find that the year 1555 – when Giorgio Vasari entered the service of Duke Cosimo I – represents a turning point in this specific area as well. While intensifying the architectural and decorative work on the Palace with the aim of making it to all effects a Medicean Ducal Palace, he also enlarged and remodelled the premises destined to serve as Wardrobe. Specifically, the radical architectural initiatives taken by Vasari starting from 1563 in the Sala Grande, today the Hall of the Five Hundred, included raising the ceiling by twelve Florentine *braccia* (about seven meters), requiring demolition of the "little rooms" existing between the trusses of the ceiling. Since these rooms had been used by the Wardrobe servants to get to *"the new Wardrobe Apartment"*, at the back of the Palace, it became necessary to build a *"little corridor"*[9] outside of it, in masonry and roofed over, leading to the other part of the Wardrobe, on the Via de' Gondi side, containing the so-called *"Crocodile Rooms*[10], due to the presence of a *"crocodile stuffed and hanging from the ceiling"*[11].

The little *corridor,* mentioned in all the inventories, was also used immediately as a place for storing and safeguarding the possessions of the court, notably some ancient marble busts. The corridor continues to appear in various 17th-18th-

[9]   ASF, Guardaroba Medicea, Inventory of Wardrobe Items formerly belonging to His Most Felicitous Grand Duke Cosimo Felice and today to His Most Serene Grand Duke Francesco de Medici taken in consignment, June 1574, f. 87, c. 67v

19th-century images, until it was demolished during the time when Florence was capital of Italy. In its place, however, there can still be seen today, on the outer wall of the Hall of the Five Hundred overlooking Via dei Gondi, a little terrace that faithfully replicates the old passageway to the Wardrobe.

Returning to the central room of the Wardrobe – that is, the Hall of Geographical Maps – we may note that two leaves of the cabinets were actually doors. One, behind the painting of the map of Italy, connected the Hall of Maps Room to the one now known as Sala della Cancelleria, or of Machiavelli; the other, behind the map of Armenia, led to the so-called Secret Wardrobe (*Guardaroba segreta*). This gave access, starting in the 1580s, to Bianca Cappello's room (*Camerino di Bianca Cappello*). This little room, its ceiling decorated in refined grotesque figures by Annibale da Campogiallo, had been built by Grand Duke Francesco I for his second wife, who used it as a studiolo in which to keep miniature artworks in her collection. The room then became, under Grand Duke Ferdinando I, the Room of Donations (*Stanzino dei donativi*[12]), where some of the gifts received from other Italian and European courts were kept.

Lastly, it should be noted that the history of the Hall of Geographical Maps, or of the Wardrobe – as has been indicated, though only schematically – is virtually paradigmatic of the more general history of the entire Ducal Palace, which – over the course of the 17th century and especially in the 18th – saw the progressive enlargement of the Medicean Wardrobe into all of its rooms; and to such an extent that in the 18th century the cabinets entirely concealed the painted histories ordered by Cosimo and realized by Giorgio Vasari in the Medici's first ducal palace, decreeing a sort of oblivion of the ducal palace itself, in whose monumental halls were stored, starting in 1720: curtains, mattresses, sedan chairs, baldachins, doors, cushions, canopies, tables and carpets… But there is one exception which, not by chance, concerns the Hall of the Five Hundred. Due to its exceptional size, it remains the only hall in Cosimo's Ducal Palace to retain importance of its own, within a Palace that has become truly *old*.

[10] Ivi, c. 58r.

[11] *Ibidem*, c. 58r.

[12] ASF, Guardaroba medicea, General Register of Wardrobe Items, February 1608 - f. 289, c. 41

Antonio di Annibale da Campogiallo, grotesque figures decorating the ceiling of the Grand Duchess Bianca Cappello's room (1581), Palazzo Vecchio

The *wonders* of the Hall of Geographical Maps in Palazzo Vecchio

G. Vasari, *Cosimo I fortifies Cosmopoli on the Island of Elba,* Hall of Cosimo I (1556), Palazzo Vecchio

Before presenting a selection from the many wonders and curiosities appearing in the maps in the Hall of Geographical Maps, we should note that, in Palazzo Vecchio, representations of the territory are found not only in the Hall of Maps, but as a basic feature of all of the painted stories, where representations of Florence, its territory and the Grand Duchy held important geo-political significance at the time, and that have today assumed great documentary value.

In the halls of the new Ducal Palace, in fact, Giorgio Vasari, with the invaluable collaboration of the Flemish artist Giovanni Stradano, painted an impressive series of images of Florence, of the towns, castles and sites of Tuscany. Outstanding among them – in the Hall of Clement VII – is the great fresco depicting the city besieged by imperial troops in 1529, a painting that is not only a faithful documentation of one of the most dramatic pages in the city's history, but also a topographical representation of Florence in the first half of the 16th century, taken *"from the band of mountains true to nature and measured in a manner very close to reality."*[13]

And it was just this vast representation of the territories of the domaine in the Palace's decorative cycle that allowed Cosimo I to chose a representation of the known world of his day, in the Hall of Geographical Maps, differing from the pictorial cycles of geographical content that, in the wake of the explorations and discoveries carried out near the end of the 15th century, began to fill the walls of rooms and galleries in some Italian palaces, most notably the Third Loggia and the Gallery of Geographical Maps in the Vatican, and the Cosmography Room in Palazzo Farnese at Caprarola.

But the Hall of Geographical Maps in Palazzo Vecchio is the oldest cycle and the only one that can be considered, in the fifty-three panels painted from 1563 to

[13] Giorgio Vasari, *Ragionamenti,* Giornata seconda, Ragionamento quarto, Florence 1588, p. 80

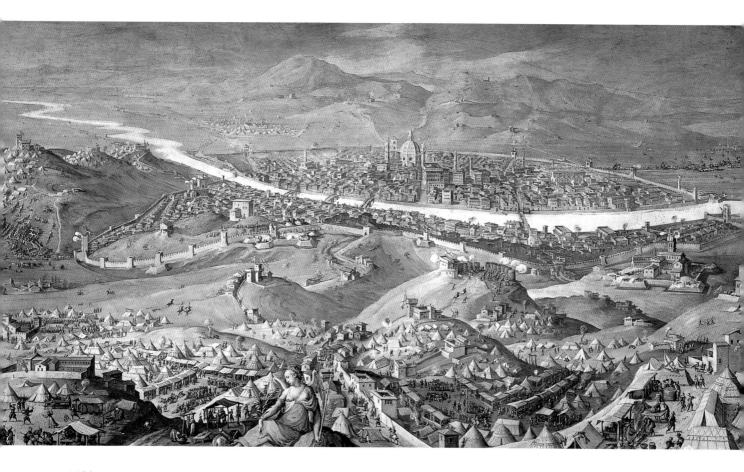

1586 – first by the Dominican Egnazio Danti and then by the Olivetan Stefano Buonsignori – as an atlas of modern times designed to reflect the sum total of the knowledge acquired by mankind,and in the meantime, to amaze visitors with the power of the *information* incorporated in the cabinet doors and with the "*extraordinary size*"[14] of the terrestrial globe built by Friar Egnazio.

    Some of the "curiosities" taken from the vast repertory of the cartouches that accompany all of the maps in the Hall of Geographical Maps are presented here.

G. Stradano, *Siege of Florence*,
Hall of Clement VII (1556-62),
Palazzo Vecchio

[14] Archive of the Uffizi Library (ABU), Inventory of the Gallery, 1704, c. 3r

Cartouche of Agisimba [Niger and Nigeria]

S. Buonsignori, Hall of Geographical Maps, Palazzo Vecchio

In the panel illustrating equatorial Africa, Stefano Buonsignori stigmatizes the learned men of his day – geographers, historians, philosophers – for having always described the most distant lands as filled with traps and danger, thus discouraging anyone from exploring them.

At the same time, however, the Olivetan geographer filled his panels of Africa and the only one dedicated to the New World – that of the Strait of Magellan – with monstrous creatures without heads, or with animal heads, dogs' heads, or half man and half animal. Buonsignori probably considered the monsters in accordance with medieval tradition, that is, as mysterious divine warnings (monstrum, from the Latin *monere*=avvisare, or warn). In this way he tried to attribute the curious, disconcerting aspects of the lands most recently discovered and explored to manifestations of Divine power, of a nature fashioned by the Creator according to inscrutable designs.

"The Geographers are accustomed to terminate the lands unknown to them with horrible wildernesses, unnavigable seas and the steepest, harshest mountains. Nor do the historians fail to help them, by describing the customs of men worse than bestial, the nature of the cruelest animals and the most dangerous impediments; with which things they hide the truth, and conceal many beautiful Lands, by depriving them of such good news and frightening men from seeking them".

Coast of China and Island of Giape, or Ciapangu [China and Japan]

E. Danti, Hall of Geographical Maps, Palazzo Vecchio

Some Far Eastern countries, such as the Archipelago of Japan, were so unreachable for occidental visitors that the geographers did not know exactly where to place them on their map. In the modern age, Japan was traditionally situated lying along the plane of the parallel, and not on the southwest/northeast axis as it is in reality. Some geographers, however, began to declare this new physical location of the island, and Egnazio Danti was aware of this. However, he designed the Island of Giape according to tradition, handed down mainly by Marco Polo's book *The Million* and the *Decades of Asia* by the erudite Portuguese João de Barros. This was in accordance with the desire of Duke Cosimo, who oversaw the execution of the entire project in the Hall and assiduously visited the young friar's place of work, as he did with all of the work involved in creating the decorative and celebratory program in Palazzo Vecchio.

"Great diversity exists among the Geographers in situating this coast of China, and the Island of Japan, which in this panel have been placed according to the opinion of the most modern scholars, although it seems that this coast should extend from Cape Liampo as far as Pangiu to the South, and to the Northwest and not to the Northeast and the East as it appears here; and the island of Japan should extend to the South and North, and not the East and West. But because in the great globe they have been situated (through the determination of His Most Serene Highness Cosimo Grand Duke of Tuscany) in the manner described by Marco Polo and the mode established by Signor Giovan di Baros".

THE HALL OF GEOGRAPHICAL MAPS

China

E. Danti, Hall of Geographical Maps, Palazzo Vecchio

In the early 16th century there existed a flourishing trade in porcelain exported from China to Europe. This porcelain was so highly appreciated that even the Western World tried to imitate its whiteness and translucence. The first experiments in this production took place in the 16th century in Italy, and most notably in Medicean Florence, in Palazzo Vecchio, in the so-called foundries, where both Cosimo and his son Francesco tried to discover the secret of Chinese porcelain. In the year when Danti wrote this recipe for manufacturing porcelain, based on a mixture of eggshells and seashells lined with mother-in-pearl, a first result, although partial, was obtained. This was one of the first examples of Medicean porcelain, made of a soft impasto, without kaolin.

"The China that was called in Antiquity the region of the Sini is inhabited by people who are in their customs and their whiteness and the quality of their bodies very similar to the Italians, but who in their dress and in the sound and pronunciation of their voices resemble the Germans. In that province are produced great quantities of Textiles made of silk and gold and of wool, and of cotton. They invented printing and artillery before us, but among other things, they produce porcelain, which contains Caracoli seashells and eggshells which they crush and mix together with other materials to form a mixture that they bury in the ground for eighty or a hundred years to refine it, and leave it to their children to finish. They have many of these holes, and as one is gradually emptied, they fill up another."

New Spain [Mexico]

E. Danti, Hall of Geographical Maps, Palazzo Vecchio

In the 16th century, the new lands discovered by Columbus near the end of the previous century, the so-called West Indies, aroused great interest. The Spanish conquistadores described fabulous cities with enormous buildings, encircled by high walls and as populous as the great European centres. This was the case of Cuzco, the Peruvian capital of the Incas, *"which is not only one of the most beautiful cities in India but could rival many cities in Italy.*

Among the largest and most important cities of this province, the great city of Mexico is supreme; it is situated in the water like Vinegia (Venice) but in a lake of water that is fresh on the Southern side where 3 big rivers flow into it and is salty from half way up, on the Northern side where the city is. In this city are 100,025 houses, as some have written, and as the aforesaid Friar Alfonso has repeatedly told me, who having seen Venice, says it is smaller than Mexico by two-thirds".

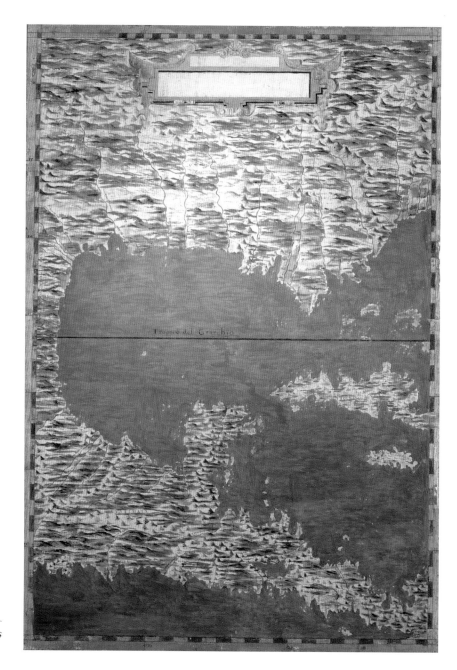

The British Isles

Land of the Troglodytes [Somalia]

S. Buonsignori, Hall of Geographical Maps, Palazzo Vecchio

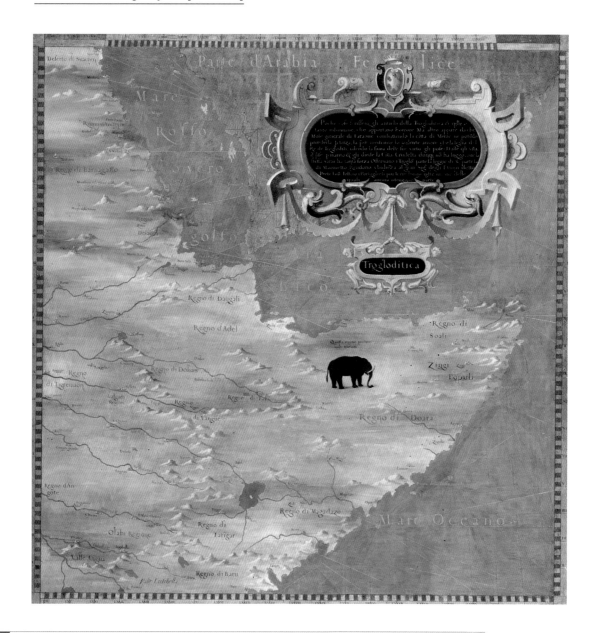

Agisimba [Niger and Nigeria] and Nubia [Sudan], details

S. Buonsignori, Hall of Geographical Maps, Palazzo Vecchio

"They also say that some who have no heads have eyes in their shoulders, and describe other characteristics of men and hominids which, taken from books of fabulous tales, have been depicted in mosaic in the port of Carthage. I would be unable to describe the cynocephalus beings, because with their dogs' heads and their barking they resemble beasts more than men". Augustine of Hippo, *de Civitate Dei contra paganos libri XXII (The City of God)* 412-426, XVI.8.1

Arabia

E. Danti, Hall of Geographical
Maps, Palazzo Vecchio

THE HALL OF GEOGRAPHICAL MAPS

The Moluccas

E. Danti, Hall of Geographical Maps, Palazzo Vecchio

Cartouche of the Island of Zeilan [Sri Lanka]

E. Danti, detail from the map of
India, Hall of Geographical Maps,
Palazzo Vecchio

West Indies [California]

E. Danti, Hall of Geographical Maps,
Palazzo Vecchio

Strait of Magellan

S. Buonsignori, Hall of Geographical Maps,
Palazzo Vecchio

Strait of Magellan, details

S. Buonsignori, Hall of Geographical
Maps, Palazzo Vecchio

Peru [Brazil], details

E. Danti, Hall of Geographical Maps, Palazzo Vecchio

"They are called cannibals, because most of this generation, if not all, live on human flesh, and you may take this for certain, Your Magnificence. They do not eat each other, but navigate in certain craft that they have, called canoes, and seek their prey on the islands and lands of a generation that is their enemy"* (from a letter by Amerigo Vespucci to Lorenzo di Pierfrancesco de' Medici, written in Cadiz on 18 July 1500 "on return from the Islands of India")

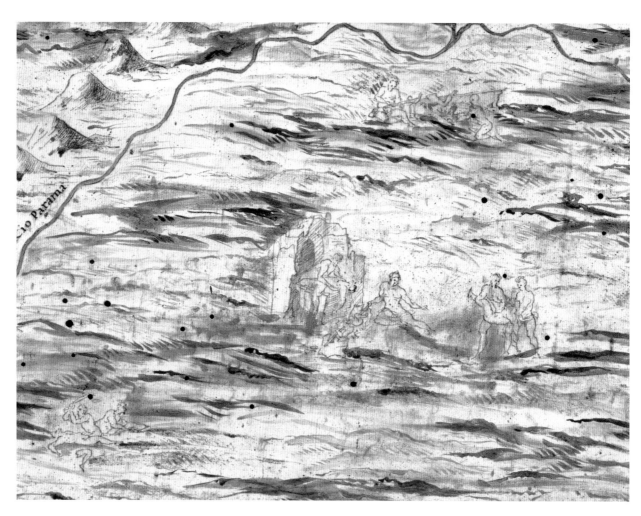

Printed in Florence
by Polistampa
in the month of November 2014